I0616900

For

Our

Children

Poems & Stories

By David Prestbury

Copyright © **David Prestbury 2009**
All rights reserved

No part of this publication
maybe reproduced,
Transmitted, utilized in any form
Or means
Without prior permission
of the publisher

All poems are by the author
(Apart from T'was Christmas day in
Workhouse (anon)
& Songs & poetry classics in which the
author has re-written

All Drawings, cartoons
Art work illustrations
Including Front cover painting
& Back cover photo taken on - Paignton
Pier, Devon, England
Are by the author

All photographs are also
By the Author
Apart from the family archive photo's

Ibsn no. 978-0-9559777-3-2

First edition 2009
Published by David Prestbury through
Lulu.com

For
My Mum
My Children
My Grandchildren
& all my fantastic family
&
great friends

This one's for you

David Prestbury 2009

Acknowledgement

I'd like to thank –

My mum, my family
Especially my children
& grandchildren
For their love & support
& most of all their inspiration
When writing this book

& I hope that this book brings
A little smile
& laughter to their lives
In this present climate
Of change, recession
& swine flu

Contents

1   *For Our Children*

3   *The Magic Spectacles*

5   *On Rescuing A Wasp*

6   *Mum's The Word*

7   *The Painted Lady*

8   *The Dragonfly*

9   *Feral Squirrel*

10 *Eric The Frog*

11 *The Woeful World Of Walter Warthog*

26 *The Rhinocerich*

27 *The Kangorillapig*

28 *Soul Mate*

29 *The Most Distinguished Bricky By Trade*

31 *I Drank It My Way*

33 *At The Co-op, Co-op in Bangor*

35 *Help Me Make it Thro' the Night(shift)*

36 *Sonnet*

37 *I Wandered Lonely As Tramp*

38 *If Only*

40 *A Little Story*

47 *We Had Nowt'*

48 *Respect*

49 *Granddad Never Spoke*

51 Whatever Happened To –

52 Lost In a Maze

53 Snow Fun

54 The Last Days of Winter

55 Holding Back

56 Life's one long Journey

57 The Spice of Life

58 Believe

59 Lazy Tongue/Err/Funny Talk

61 The Man Who Knew

62 Faces

66 Haunted

68 Seasons – Spring Time

69 Summertime

70 Autumn Time

71 The Dancing Trees

72 Winter Time

73 That's Life

74 T'was Christmas Day

75 Land of Hope &Tory

76 David Prestbury

77 Dave's Books

For Our Children

I remember when
You were little children
Your first days at school
Taking you to your first movies

Walt Disney cartoons
Loony Tunes
With plenty of treats -
Ice-cream, popcorn & *Haribo* sweets

Wide-eyed & mesmerized
Oh! How you cried & cried
When Bambi's mum
Got shot & died

And at that ever so sad scene
When Snow white collapsed & died
After eating that poisoned apple given to her
By that wicked Witch of a Queen

Then came back alive
When given that magical kiss of life
By the handsome young Prince
Oh! How you sighed!

And how you would wail
Until Pinocchio & his father Geppetto
Escaped from inside Monstro
That terrifying gigantic Whale

And how you all got angry & mad
At Tinkerbelle's jealous betrayal
Of Peter Pan & Cinderella
By her ugly sisters, that made you all so sad

But it all came right in the end
When they all lived happily ever after
As you skipped all the way home holding
Hands singing Jiminy Cricket's song -

'When you wish upon a star
Makes no difference who you are
When you wish upon a star
Your dreams come true'

Those were happy days
To look back upon
When you were innocent
So innocent little children

The Magic Spectacles

Not so long ago
& not so far away
Lived a special boy
Who one fine day

Received an unexpected package
From the village Postman, Mr. Pugh -
Who it was from -
Nobody knew?

& when he opened it - to his surprise
Was a pair of 'Spectacles?'
For his short sighted eyes!
But these weren't ordinary Spectacles

They were 'Magic Spectacles'
Because they adjusted immediately
To his weakened eyes
& not only that –

He could adjust them to see into the future
& he could see into the past
"Wow!" He shouted with great joy
"I could have real fun with these, Oh! Boy!"

So off he went – to adventures new
To check out the past & the future too
The past he saw - was War after War
The future quite different -Peace everywhere

With harmony at last,
Every country in tune
Without avarice & greed
Sharing the wealth & no countries to feed

A paradise World
Was being unfurled
In heavenly bliss
A state of happiness

& so it now seems
That there's hope in our dreams
A future so bright
From a past full of hate

This vision of the future his eyes see
Thro' these magical lenses, this prophesy
This mystery gift of 'magic spectacles'
Where they came from nobody knew?

Unless you know something - well do you?

On Rescuing a Wasp

On rescuing a Wasp
From a Spider's Web –
Hands on hips in a hissy fit
The Spider cried – "you silly ol' git!"

That was my dinner
And no thanks to you
I'm now much thinner
You big piece of poo!!

I'll have to weave my web again
It's enough to drive a Spider insane
The Wasp waved goodbye & buzzed off by
With a sting in his tale & a wink in his eye

Mum's the Word

The slithering, slimy & silvery trails
Left by an army of garden snails
Munching there way through their '5 a day'
Waiting for mum to show them the way

But mum was shell shocked
With what she saw
When they formed this awesome display –
That truly made her day!

The Painted Lady

Is a welcoming sight
To anyone's garden
With its colours so bright

Flittering & fluttering
Spending hours upon hours
Sipping nectar from
Its favourite flowers

The Dragonfly

The Dragonfly –
Looks a fearsome sight
When fluttering it's wings
Like a helicopter in flight

Large hawkers & little darters
With fierce jaws & huge eyes
Go hunting for prey –
Mosquitoes, small insects & annoying flies

But this one I see
Is waving at me
- What do you think?
(Or is it the drink!)

Feral Squirrel

Feral Squirrel foraging free
Around the garden & up the tree

Onto the bird table, nibbling nuts & seeds
Anything edible, for his hibernating needs

Eric the Frog

Eric the lazy little Frog
Was sleeping like a leftover log

Then went absolutely crazy
Croaking his little head off

Hopping mad & getting quite perturbed
When he was inconveniently disturbed

From his afternoon nap
By this little photo snap!

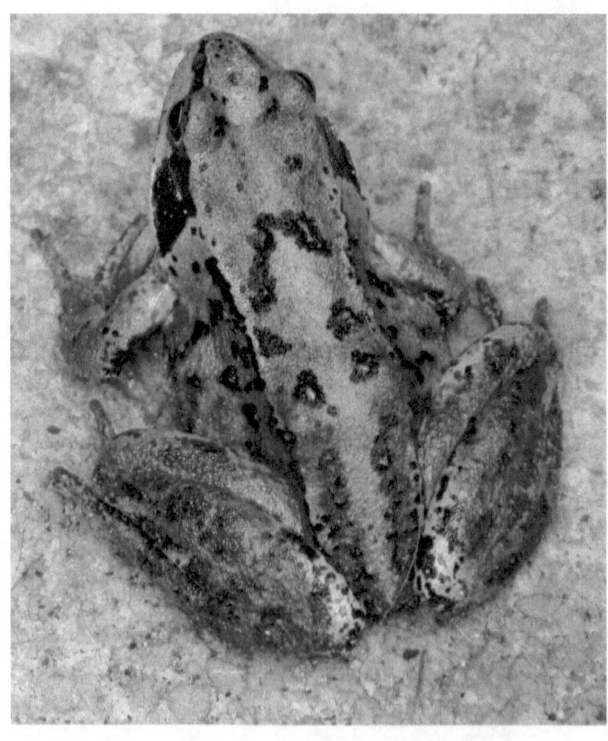

The Woeful World
of
Walter Warthog

Part one

Grumble in the Jungle

'Why! Oh! Why! Am I so ugly?'
Whined Walter Warthog,
'Just look at my phizzog & physique –

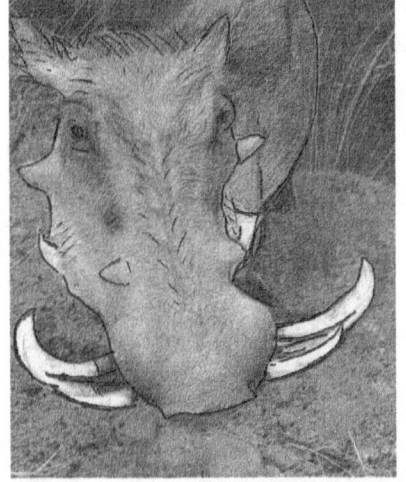

Mother Nature could have made me:
As handsome as a Horse
As stunning as a Stag
As pretty as a Panther
As rip-roaring as a Lion
As tenacious as a Tiger
As fearsome as a Frog (maybe not!)
But she made me into some kinda freak!'

'Ha! Ha! Ha!'Laughed Albert Alligator
Flashing his impeccable teeth

'What's up Croc?' Croaked Horace Hippo
'Ooh! You are such a Boar Walter Warthog'
Yyyawned! Horace Hippo & fell fast asleep

'Accept yourself for what you are,
You were born with that ugly muzzle
& you can't do a thing about it',
Ranted Robert Rhino as he arrogantly
Crossed his eyes

To admire his large white horn,
'They pay an absolute fortune for these,
You know - Vanity Hunters –
To use as an aphrodisiac or something!'

Then Zeke the Zebra chip's in with
'They named a 'crossing' after me he-he!
'& I, had a poem written 'bout me',
Boasted Tyrone Tiger –'by William Blake –
Tiger! Tiger! Burning bright
In the Forests of the night."

'Ok! Ok! Enough is enough' William Blake
- For God's sake', wailed Walter,

'Wwhat about plastic surgery?'
Enthused Walter,
In an uninspiring tone of voice,
'I know a Proboscis Monkey,
Who had a nose-job
But it cost a few bob',

'Der! Did sompbody call be?'
Snouted a certain Snub-nosed Monkey
(Who looked more like Jack Palance
Than Jack Palance)

'I was enquiring about your nose-job',
Said Walter in a slightly embarrassed way'
'Dow my dew dose!' laughed Snoz
The Snub-Nosed Monkey, with great pride

'Stop splashing me with your tail,
You're getting my shell suit all mucky',
Bitched Tommy Turtle,
In his unusual sort of way.

'How much did you pay the Snub-Nosed
Monkey Surgeon? probed an over excited
Walter -'Doo undred bounds!' snouted Snoz

'Walnuts!!' cried Walter,
'I dow but it bos borth it,

All der Baboons fancy me dow!!
Any bay I have to go dow dy! dy!'
So off Snoz goes admiring his dew dose

'Snod dat! I mean 'that'
For two penny Monkey's', Quipped Walter,
Having a quick roll in the mud.

'Ouch! Yah! Big ugly oaf!'
Growled Horace Hippo

'Sssorry!' Whimpered Walter
In his pathetic cowering way

As Peter Parrot prattles & squawks -
This is true! - This is true!
Walter Warthog! Walter Warthog!
You look like poo! - You look like poo!

This tickled Charlie the Chimpanzee
Who was chuckling & chattering to himself
& eating a Flee

'By the way have you seen Colin Cobra
Recently?' snorted Horace Hippo
He was last seen hissing
About The Jungle
Three Monsoons ago,
Guffawed Gerald Giraffe,
With his head in the
Clouds,

'Oh! That slithering,
Son of a Rattlesnake,
The last time I heard
Penelope Python had a
Crush on him!'

'Ha! Ha! Ha!' Laughed Walter
At his sick sense of humour.

'Oh! You boring old swine,'
Yyyawned! Horace Hippo
Once again & fell fast asleep

'Cobras! To you Horace Hippo –
You hippo-crit', wittered Walter .

'Sssh!' Shushed Sam the Sloth slouching &
Dangling upside down on his favourite tree

'Tusk! Tusk! Tusk!' Tusked Elle Elephant,
Blowing her own trumpet as usual as she
Tramped & trumpeted by.

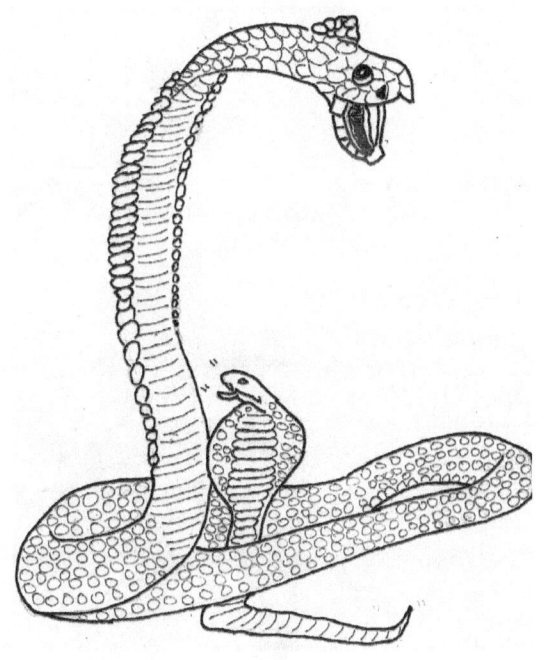

So off Walter waddles,
'I think I'll have a word with the King,
Perhaps he'll give me some reassurance?'

'Lionel! Lionel! Are you there?'
'Rrrrrroar!! Roared Lionel Lion
'Have you a minute?' Pleaded Walter.
'Who keeps blarting?
Is it that
Trumped up villain
Elle the Elephant?
Growled Lionel,

'I'll be back in a Whisker
so make it Snappy I've an appointment with
the Mane dresser
In ten minutes – I'm having a perm!'

'It's about my
Appearance',
Groaned Walter in his
Inferior sort of way

'Oh! I see,
'Just 'cos yer face is
Like a Baboon's bum
With hemorrhoids!!
Growled Lionel'

'I'm off to feast on a Passing Wildebeest
Or Three 'Yum-Yum-Yum!'
Slavered Lionel lickin' his lips

'Oh! Dear! Dear! Dear!me',
Uttered Deirdrie Deer
Then fled for her life - instantly

'There you go mocking me.,
Oh! You're just like all the others,' sobbed
Walter feeling so affected –
'Oh! What can I do? Sob! Sob!

'Commit Hari Kari! Advised Lionel
In his usual heartless way,'

'I think I'll throw myself under
Elle Elephant!'Cried Walter
Still sob sobbin'.

'Boom! Boom! Boom! what's all this
Sobbin' About?' Grunted Garth
Gorilla

As he swung his way from his tree
Nutting a coca-nut in half!

'Swing along with Garth pal
& I'll teach you knowledge
That will help you pass your 'Ape Levels'

Then you can look down on all these dumb
Animals & reign superior, come take my
Hand & I'll swing you to 'the learning tree'

'Sounds all Hogwash to me,'
Grunts Walter.

'Don'tcha! Mean Gorilla guff!'
Huffed & puffed Lionel,
Who was panting away?
From chasing his prey.

'Sssh!' shushed Walter ,
'He might stick the nut on me!
Any way
I'll think I'll go & gather
A few berries for Tea,'-
Walter declares

So off Walter waddles,
Muttering & wittering
To himself,
Passing a crowd
Of chattering,
Chimps chomping on Bananas & nuts
Along the way.

Rumble in the Jungle

Part two

'I suppose if I was a Human, I'd look like
Marty Feldman or something,'
Come to think of it –
Even He makes me look handsome!
I know! If I keep saying to myself –

'Warts are wonderful, warts are Devine,
It's so special to be a swine!
A beautiful Boar is what I'll be
Marty Feldman is uglier than me!

'I might gain myself some slutch courage,
Then I can go trapping off & try to ensnare
myself a few Brazen Hoggies',

'Aye! I must trot off now to mi local
Watering hole - to trim mi whiskers,
Preen & polish mi warts,
Then I'll try one at'Ye old Boar's Head'
Then 'The Tooth & Claw'
& then it's off to -
'The Cat's Whisker' Discotèque where I can
Hog the dance floor then get up onto the
Stage to sing my favourite karaoke song' –

'I'm a Hog for you baby
I can't get enough of your lurrve
When I go to sleep at night
You're the only sow I'm thinkin' orrrf'

'I'll have all those sexy sows
Screeching after me!
Yeh! Baby! I'll suppose
I'll become a Super Hog
'Oink! Oink! Oink! Laughs
Walter in his new found egocentric way -
'I'll become a real Chauvinist pig then',

'I can just see myself on the Telly –
'Tonight fffrom –
'The Cat's Whisker'Discoteque
In the deepest, darkest (& daftest?) Jungle –

'Walter Winston Warthog! –
This is your Lioffe!
I can just see Aemon Antelope's face now!

'Oh! Well I must stop all this daydreaming
& fantasizing, it's making me go all giddy',
I'm off for a few beers to cheer myself up

'Hey just look who's over there –
Behind the Bar
It's only - the one & only!-
Wwwanda Warthog!

I haven't seen her since she was
A little Hoglet – Wow! She's beautiful!
B-b-but how can a Warthog be beautiful?
It doesn't make sense? Or does it?

Whatever, she's smiling at me –
I-I-I think she fancies me,

Well who'd have thought it?
'Come to daddy! Wanda baby
Gizza a hog er I mean a hug,
Let's lock horns, kiss warts
& make beautiful little Hoggies together,'

So off Walter & Wanda waddle
To their fairytale wedding day
& what a celebration & commotion
There was
A right ol' 'Rumble in the Jungle' that day!

& I have to say that beauty is
Certainly in the eye
Of the Beer holder
Er! I mean beholder
& they both lived
Hoggily er -I mean
Happily ever after

The End (or is it?)

The Rhinocerich

What a daft wretch
Is the Rhinocerich
She rolls about in mud & muck
Buries her head (for good luck)
& always gets her horn stuck!!

The Kangorillapig

Is one of the strangest
Animals that you'll ever see
He hops, then jumps, grunts & snorts

Then swings & hits a tree!!

Soul Mate

You have the rhythm
I have the beat

You send shivers
Down to my feet

You have the rock
I have the roll

We have the music
In our soul

He's the Most Distinguished
Bricky By Trade

He's the most distinguished Bricky by trade
Has nowt in his pocket 'til he gets paid

Then it's off to his local –
In Wellington's & cap
For a quick game of darts
Sups ten pints of Lager
& has the odd scrap

Then off to the Bookies
(Turf accountants if you're posh!)
For an each way bet on a tipped horse
An odds on cert. - he loses his dosh
& comes out cursing without his shirt on!

He's the most distinguished Bricky by trade
Has nowt in his pocket 'til he gets paid

Then he's off on the tap to try & get laid
At the working men's club - down the Lane
He cops for a floozy
('cos he aint that choosey)
& he gets a good slap for being too cheeky

He's the most distinguished Bricky by trade
Has nowt in his pocket 'til he gets paid
Then he crawls to the Chippy
For meat pie & chips

Off home he staggers & throws up his guts
Fast asleep in his chair –
With bits of carrots in his hair

He's the most distinguished Bricky by trade
Has nowt in his pocket 'til he gets paid

Gets up to a hangover & off to the site
Chucks up in his mix, not a pretty site
This boy wonder then trowels in his chunder
As sick as a brick as the lads take the mick

Now -
He's the most 'extinguished' Bricky by trade
Has nowt in his pocket until he gets paid

I Drank It My Way

I know it'll end in tears
& so I face the final curtain
My friend, ol' Boddingtons beer
I'll sup a crate, to which I'm certain

I've lived a life that's full
I've staggered each & every pub doorway
Lot's more lot's of this
I drank it my way

Cigarettes I've had a few
But then again to few to mention
I drank what I had to drink
& supped it down without intervention

I planned each charted course
Each Boddingtons Pub along the roadway
Lot's more lot's more than this
I drank it my way

Yes, there were times, I'm sure you knew
That I drank more that I could too
But thro' it all, when there was Stout
I threw it up & spat it out
I faced it all & supped more
& drank it my way

I've loved, I've laughed & cried
I've had my share of boozing
& now as with beer & pies
I find it all so amusing

To think I drank all that
& may I say not in a shy way
No, oh no not me
I drank it my way

For what is a man, what has he got?
If not himself then he has his pint pot
To slur the things he truly feels
& not the word of one who keels
The drunken shows I took the blows
& drank it my way

By Paul Tankard

32

At the Co-op, Co-op in Bangor

Her name was Dora, she was a salesgirl
With yellow streaks run thro' her hair
& a dress cut down to dare
She would moan & argue
& do the checkout
& while she tried to be a star
Taffy saw she wore no bra.
Across a crowded store
They worked from 9 to 4
They were young & had each other
& she would ask for more?

At the Co-op, Co-op in Bangor
The cheapest shop north of Lake Bala
At the Co-op, Co-op in Bangor
Taped music & passion
Were always the fashion
At the Co-op – They fell in love

His name was Ricardo
He wore an Alice band
He was seduced to a stare
When he saw Dora bending there
& when she gave a flash
He drooled allover her
But Ricardo went a bit too far
Taffy skated across the store
& then he punched in the jaw
Heads were smashed in two
There was blood & there was snot
But who's snot who's

At the Co-op, Co-op in Bangor
The cheapest shop north of Lake Bala
At the Co-op, Co-op in Bangor
Taped music & passion
Were always the fashion
At the Co-op – they fell in love

At the Co-op (scream)
She lost her job
Co-op, Co-op in Bangor
Her name was Dora
She was a salesgirl
But that was 9 months ago
When she used to have a glow
Now it's a Tesco, but not for Dora
Now in a dress from mothercare
With faded highlights in her hair
She lost her virginity
& she lost her Taffy
Now she's lost her mind

At the Co-op, Co-op in Bangor
The cheapest shop north of Lake Bala
At the Co-op, Co-op in Bangor
Taped music & passion
Were always the fashion
At the Co-op – Don't fall in love
                Don't fall in love
                Co-op in Bangor
                Co-op in Bangor
                Co-op in Bangor

By Manny Barrylow

Help Me Make it Thro' the Night (shift)

Shake the dandruff from my hair
Shake it loose & let it fall
Scratch the stubble from my chin
See the shadows under my eyeballs

Get my head down & try to hide
Until the early mornin' shift
All I'm takin' is your time (& half)
Help me make it thro' the night (shift)

I don't care if my social life's gone
I don't try to keep awake
Let the Devil take tomorrow
For tonight I need a sleep

Yesterday is dead & gone
& tomorrow's my last night
It's so great to gerroff home
Help me make it thro' the night
(shift)

by (notso)Gladit's Nights & the Kips

Sonnet

Shall I compare thee to a winter's day?
Thou art more slovenly & more desperate
Wild winds shake the snarling woods of day
& winter's lease hath all too short of date
Sometimes too cold the eye of glass shines
& often is his grim complexion dammed
& every hair from head sometimes declines
By chance of his minging face untrimmed
But thy eternal winter shall not fade
Nor lose obsession of the hair thou loses
Nor shall death drag thou cursed in his shade
With facial lines & in no time thou greyest

So long as men deceive & evil eye can see
So long lives this & this give strife to thee

By Sillyman Shakesrear

36

I Wandered Lonely as a Tramp

I wandered lonely as a Tramp
 That trudges over derelict sites & dumps
When all at once I saw a mound -
 A cluster of golden Buttercups
Beside the puddles, beneath the trees,
Stuttering & prancing in the breeze.

Continuous as the cats eyes that shine
 & twinkle on the motorway,
They stretched in never ending line
 Along the side of mud & clay;
Ten thousand saw I at a glance,
Nodding their heads in unsightly stance.

The Graves beside them danced; but they
 Outdid the morbid Graves in glee;
A poet could not but be gay,
 In such a joke of company;
I gazed - & gazed - but little thought
What bad health the show
To me had brought;

For oft, when on my couch I lie
 In vagrant or in pensive mood,
They flash upon that inward eye
 With this misery of solitude;
And then my hand with Whiskey sups,
And staggers with the Buttercups.

By William Jobsworth

If Only

If only
You can keep your hair
When all about you are losing theirs
& blaming it on cheap shampoo,

If only
You can brace yourself
When all mums clout you.
But make allowances for their shouting too;

If only
You can want & not be tired of wanting.
Or being a layabout, don't deal in lie-ins
Or being hated, don't give way to hating,
& yet don't look too good nor eat all the pies

If only
You can dream & not make dreams your waster;

IF only
You can think & not make thoughts your blame

If only
You can meet with triumph & disaster
& treat those two imposters just the same

If only
You can dare to hear the truth you've broken
Twisted by lies to make a mockery of rules
Or watch the things you gave your life to, stolen,
And smack & beat them with worn out tools;

If only
You make one heap of all your winnings
& risk it on one lame horse & lose & start again,
Losing all your savings
& never breathe a word about your loss;

If only
You can cook a Heart or Barley stew
To serve for lunch after they've gone,
To eat when there's nothing inside you
Except the will which says to them do one!

If only
You can talk with clowns & keep you humour,
Or walk with Kings –
Nor lose the common 'as muck' touch

If only
Neither foes nor loathing fiends can hurt you,

If only
You can fill the unforgiving minute
With sixty seconds worth of instant fun,

Yours is the Earth & every worm that's in it,
& which is more – you've been had my son!

By Ruddy Wellard Crippling

A Little Story

One bright, cheerful, sunny autumn's day.
Two little children called Robyn & Charlie
along with their Mummy Lisa & Daddy
Nick, went to visit their great Nana Win.
Who lived only a couple of streets away
from where they lived in the suburban area
of Failsworth, in Greater Manchester.

They liked to visit their great Nana Win
on Sundays - to hear her old stories about the
War time years - these stories used to excite,
fascinate & captivate them.

They also liked to play in great Nana's
beautiful back garden which was full of
pretty colourful flowers, shrubs & trees.
Sometimes they would collect snails &
insects & run around the lawn exploring
& counting the many garden ornaments that
great Nana collected over the years.

This particular hazy, lazy day they were
running around playing tig when
Charlie who was always very mischievous
& had the cheekiest of faces, accidentally
knocked over one of the stone ornaments,
which happened to be a Bird Bath,

Robyn, being a really pretty little girl
with long blond hair & big blue eyes
Shouted loudly at Charlie –
Charlie! Charlie! You idiot!!

A 'Trap door' suddenly appeared
- as if by some kind of magic! -
Directly underneath the Bird Bath -
Revealing these dusty old wooden steps
that led down to an old –
'Anderson air raid shelter'.

So Robyn & Charlie being curious
Seven & eight year olds (like children do).
Went down these dusty old steps,
Only to discover this musty old air raid
shelter went back in time!

They could see a family from the 1940's
& hear sirens & bombs going off -
but nobody could see or hear them!

Although this was frightening for them,
They were both very excited,
Robyn gave a little giggle as
Charlie flicked a spider off the wall.

An old Wireless was playing old
War songs like, 'We'll meet again' &
'The white cliffs of Dover', Robyn shrugged
her shoulders, Charlie gave a little cough.

Meanwhile their Daddy Nick went looking
for them, wondering where they were,
Mummy Lisa was calling out for them too!
But they couldn't hear her, they were too
busy listening to the people in the shelter,
laughing, joking, singing & shouting.

They were also fascinated by the people's
funny clothes & hairstyles. The shelter was
like a long tunnel with people on either side.

They very carefully walked down to the end
of the tunnel & up some steps & could see
German War planes
flying high above the clouds.

From a distance they could see clouds of
black smoky fires & hear very loud blasts &
bangs. It wasn't a pretty sight which they
found quite scary & terrifying.

Robyn grabbed hold of Charlie's hand &
pulled him back inside the shelter.

Back inside the shelter which was kind of
cozy, safe & warm, they saw the look of
horror on the peoples faces, this made them
think & realize what these War time people
had gone through! –

Robyn smiled at a little boy she thought
was cute but unfortunately the little boy
couldn't see her.

She also noticed a young teenage couple
holding hands & cuddling up to each other,
She was pretty with fair hair & green eyes.
He was handsome with dark auburn curly
hair & brown eyes.
They looked very much in love.

Charlie panicked & tugged Robyn
he wanted to go back up into the garden.

So back up the dusty old wooden steps
they climbed, they could see their Mummy
& Daddy searching frantically for them.

They lifted the trap door open & pushed the
Bird Bath back, then skipped around behind
the shady trees, dusting themselves down,
then shouted & waved at their Mummy &
Daddy who were ever so relieved to see
them!

Then they excitingly tried to explain their
adventure to their Mummy, Daddy & great
Nana but unfortunately they could see that
they weren't convincing them –
Who thought it was only make believe!

When all was quiet,
great Nana got some old photographs out
for them to look at.

Robyn was startled by photo's
of great Nana & great Granddad -
that were taken many years ago,
because they looked identical to the young
couple that she saw in the air aid shelter!

Robyn never said anything
but looked at great Nana,
who smiled back at her & gave her a wink!

We Had Nowt'

Mum always says –
We had nowt' but we were 'appy
In days gone by
In war time years

Those Dancehall days
The big Band sounds
Piano's played in Parlours
Sing-along in Pubs

Goin' to the Flicks
Mangles & Dolly tubs
When Rations
Was the unfortunate Fashion

Wearing Mum's ol' shoes
& Granny's shawl
Kickin' a Casey
Against a backyard wall

Air raid shelters in back gardens' & crofts
Black outs & sirens,
Bombs dropping on factories, houses & pubs
Explosions, The Blitz on our towns & Cities

With devastating deaths,
Tragedies & atrocities
But we all pulled together far & wide
With great community spirit
& most of all Great British pride

Respect

You, young people
That mock & laugh
At the elderly
Spare a thought & listen

They were once like you, full of fun,
Mischievous, having a lark
& played the fool
Went to School,

Left School at fourteen on into work
On munitions, the Home guard , Land Army
Called up in the Forces to fight a War
To hold a gun
& save our country From the Hun

Kinfolk died,
Families cried
Living in poverty, people were poor
Times were tough throughout the War

So never mock & laugh at old people,
Old Soldiers, you must show respect
Just remember what they went through
Because without them you wouldn't be here

To laugh, mock & jeer
Just remember one day, you'll be old too
Then how would you feel,
Well how would you?

Granddad Never Spoke

Granddad never spoke
About the Great War
The 1914-18 War
The War to end Wars

Battle torn soldiers
Entrenched, soaked in blood, mud & sludge
Amongst the dying and dead
They wearily trudged

Waiting for the call
To go over the top
On into battle, picked off and shot
For who & for what?

The Royal Welsh Fusiliers
Were his regiment
Duped into call up by the powers that be
Young so young and much too blind to see

That suicidal 'Somme'
Was a Graveyard for our Tommies
Badly wounded in his arm, but he survived
Not so his mates who perished & died

Horrific atrocities,
Memories never to be cherished
A generation extinguished, lost & buried
Flowers on their graves
The young innocent and brave

Like lambs to the slaughter
Leaving loved ones to grieve
This wasteful War –
Granddad never spoke of
Because his silence said it all

The Royal Welsh Fusiliers 1914 – 18
(Granddad 1st left - middle row)

Whatever Happened To –

Whatever happened to –
The girls you once knew

The faces, the places
You once knew?

Fading memories
Out of view!

& before you know it
Time is upon you

Looking back
Flickering through

Your life as it was
Wondering where the time was lost

Where are they now?
Do they think of you & wonder too?

Where you are going
What you are doing

& saying - whatever happened too?

Lost in a Maze

Can't find my way out
Can't figure it out

Show me the way
My minds in a whirl

It's always like this
When I meet a new girl

Snow Fun

I like to swirl
& whirl around
Then lie like a snow
Virgin on the
ground
When there's
No one to trudge
& turn me to slush
I like to be a
Snowman as such

With a nice old hat,
A carrot for a nose
Buttons for eyes, a pipe,
Scarf & mittens to pose!
I don't ask for much
Until that hazy, lazy sly old Sun

Suddenly appears,
From out of the clouds & spoils my fun
& maliciously melts my existence to mush
With nothing left of me but slush

The Last Days of Winter

Our frost frozen faces began to thaw
The animals from hibernation
Were coming to ground

A dog licked a melted icicle on the floor
The melting ice withdrew its
Pretty patterns from the streets of our town

The odd sprinkle of snow made its final fall
Shivering shoots push through
The softening soil without sound

The welcoming of spring was coming to call
Weaving its magic wand & waving goodbye
To this winter wonderland

Holding Back

Keep your feet on the ground
Keep your opinions to yourself
Keep your eyes open & your mouth shut
Keep a low profile

Keep mum
Know who you are
Be down to earth
Be who you are

Come down off that high horse
Come follow me
Don't get ideas above your station
Don't have your head in the clouds

Don't live in cloud cuckoo land
Don't get your hopes up high
Don't rock the boat
Don't create ripples

Don't push the boat out
Don't travel too far
Remember your roots
Remember where you came from

So stay where you are & don't move
& don't do one!

Life's one Long Journey
(So enjoy the ride)

When you come to the end
Of life's long journey & reflect upon
What you took from life
And gave in return & so on

From your friends
& acquaintances who
With your family & children
Cherished & loved you

To say 'hand on heart'
That you gave your all & did your best
(Maybe could have done better!)
With a clear conscience
You can peacefully rest

The Spice of Life

Unfortunately
It seems that 'notoriety'
Not 'variety' is the real spice of life
In this sick society

Believe

To all Religions of the World
Embrace yourselves

The Muslim & the Jew
The Buddhist, Sikh & Hindu
The Catholic & Protestant
& the many Denominations & cults too

Keep the peace & end the wars
Learn to respect & love each other
Don't lose the faith
That your Gods have in you

Try to reach out to one & other
Gain common ground
With your all spiritual leaders
Instead of fighting one & other

You must realize
& open your eyes
Enlighten your minds
Believe in the wisdom of the wise

Nurture nature for all mankind
If not for yourself
Learn to give & take
- For your own God's sake!

Lazy Tongue

Whatever happened too?
The English language we once knew?

The 'tee aitches' (TH) -
The becomes de
These becomes dese
Those becomes does
This becomes dis
That becomes dat
Them becomes dem

With becomes wiv or wid
Think becomes fink
Nothing becomes nuffin or nothink
Thanks becomes fanks
Together becomes togever
Everything becomes everyfin
Month becomes monf

& it gets worse when -
Other becomes uvva or udder
Bother becomes bovver or bodder
& it loses the meaning when -
Thought becomes fought

Then you've got a 'T' that becomes 'C'
When Hospital becomes Hospical
& digital becomes digical

Then 'H' becomes redundant when -
Hat becomes at
Hate become ate
Hard becomes ard

Not forgetting the 'R's that become 'W's
Sorry becomes sowwy
Great become gweat
Right become wight
As per Jonafan Woss (Jonathan Ross)
& the cast of East Enders

& it's a bit embarrassing when the
East & West Europeans speak better English
Than what we 'duz'

Err

Being a writer & versifier
There's nothing quite worse
Than a misspelling, a misprint
Or leaving out the occasional letter or word
In an all important verse

Funny talk

Dialogue with dialect, slang & lingo
Accents & drawl in our choice of languish
Gives character & charisma
With comical undertones
To our Queen's English

The Man Who Knew Everything?

He was the man
Who knew everything?

Whatever was said?
Whatever was stressed?

He was the man
Who knew the best?

Whatever you did
Whatever you've done

He would do better
He was the fitter & he always won

He was the man
Who was second to none?

There was nothing
He couldn't do

He was perfect
In everyway

Could this man
Be you???

Faces

The face in the flower is
following you

The face in the sand is
spying on you

The Tree faces are
Tracking you

<<<<<<<<<<<<<<<<Keep looking
behind you
>>>>>>>>>>>>>Someone is
pursuing you?
Is this *paranoia* consuming you?

Haunted

There's movement in the bedroom
Shadows changing shape
In this eerie darkness of the night
I cannot, cannot escape

Maybe I imagine what I see?
A Dream - a Nightmare perhaps?
But something moved, slowly creeping
Scaring the hell out of me!

I go undercover
With my head under the pillow
Can't get me now!
I reassure myself somehow

Then nervously I switch on my bedside light
- To make it disappear
Into this lonely night,
This lonely night of fear

But when I switch it off again
It's back to haunt & taunt me
Almost driving me insane
& giving me one hell of a fright

'Who are you?'
'What are you?'
'Are you a restless spirit?'
'Are you in limbo?'

'What do you want from me?'
'Please let me sleep in peace
& for God's sake -
Let me be

Seasons

Spring time

Spring awakening from winter's big sleep
From hibernation, tiny heads slowly peep
Daffodils dance in formation & droves
Tulips & primroses in full repose

Hours upon hours
Of April showers
Fall between the smiling Sun
- A new life has just begun

Summertime

Summertime brings an array of flowers
Roses rambling along the hedgerows
Trees & shrubs as tall as towers
Birds twitter & chirp in tune
Life is in the fullest bloom

Autumn time

The silent season of decay
Flowers & shrubs, sadly fading
away
Leaves from trees in freefall
Floating & gliding in the autumn
breeze
In this season of the fall

Inspiring this canvas of abstract
patterns
Of scattered leaves -
A mix of burnt orange, russet &
amber gold
For poets & artists to uphold

The Dancing Trees

Go bark-raving mad!
As they dance & sway
Then shed their leaves
Exposing themselves
In a bark-naked display

Wintertime

A cold frost freezing, snow falling scene
Creating a cloak for the shivering trees
Powdery footprints & snowmen appear
Then suddenly & sadly they all disappear

The little Robin makes
His seasonal appearance
Singing Christmas carols
Putting in his usual best performance

The children & parents twinkling faces
Glitter like tinsel
Brightening & enlightening
Another year's ending
On a memorable & magical Christmas day

That's Life

Childhood; naive, innocent & new
Youth; uncouth & callow too
Middle age; toil & strife
Old age; regret
& overrated too!
But sadly that's my life
How about you?

T'Was Christmas Day

T'was Christmas day
In the Workhouse
The **snow** was **raining** fast
A **barefooted** boy with **clogs** on
Stood lying in the grass

(Dad used to recite this little Poem
To us kids when we were little)

Land of Hope & Tory

Land of hope & Tory
Order of the Gentry

How shall thee exploit me
Who was spawned of thee

Wider still & wider
Shall thy bounds be set

Gawd, who made thee greedy
Make thee greedier yet

Gawd, who made thee greedy
Make thee greedier yet

David Prestbury

David Prestbury *was born in Great Ancoats,*
Manchester, England in 1948
he lives in Failsworth, Manchester
also has an apartment in the
Radius,Prestwich. Manchester

has been married twice has three sons,
a Daughter & two grandchildren

He's currently a full time carer
(for his sick mother)
a Landlord & full time Writer

This book is Dave's forth book
The others being –
The Donkey Stone & Dolly Blue Days
(about growing up & street life in the late
1950' & early 1960's Manchester

Oasis & the Twisted Wheel *about the*
vibrant club scene,
in sexy 1960's Manchester

& Hidden By The Clouds *sweet & sour*
Poetry love lost, love regained

DAVE'S PUBLISHED BOOKS -

Available online from Amazon.co.uk, W H Smith, Waterstones, Barnes &Noble & Borders

www.ingramcontent.com/pod-product-compliance
Lightning Source LLC
Chambersburg PA
CBHW030540180626
46810CB00005B/1951